Teid

CW00736090

Las Cañadas del Teide
National Park

Editorial Everest would like to thank you for purchasing this book. It has been created by an extensive and complete publishing team made up of photographers, illustrators and authors specialised in the field of tourism, together with our modern cartography department. Everest guarantees that the contents of this work were completely up to date at the time of going to press, and we would like to invite you to send us any information that helps us to improve our publications, so that we may always offer QUALITY TOURISM.

QUALITY
TOURISM
WITH
EVEREST

Please send your comments to:
Editorial Everest. Dpto. de Turismo
Apartado 339 – 24080 León (Spain)
Or e-mail them to us at turismo@everest.es

Editorial Management: Raquel López Varela

Editorial coordination: Eva María Fernández

Text: Francisco Javier Macías Martín

Photographs: José Luis Rodríguez, Justino Díez, Oliviero Daidola and Paolo Tiengo

Diagrams: Mercedes Fernández

Cover design: Alfredo Anievas

Digital image processing: David Aller

Translation: EURO:TEXT, Martin Gell

© EDITORIAL EVEREST, S. A.
Carretera León-La Coruña, km 5 – LEÓN
ISBN: 84-241-0226-6
Legal deposit: LE. 732-2001
Printed in Spain

EDITORIAL EVERGRÁFICAS, S. L.
Carretera León-La Coruña, km 5
LEÓN (Spain)

Teide

Tenerife, with an area of 2,057 km², is the largest of the Canary Islands. It has a very rugged landscape and is noted for a mountainous backbone that runs across it from north-east to south-west. The large volcanic Las Cañadas cauldron crowns this wild division. A large volcanic cone, the Pico del Teide, rises out of it and its summit is at 3,717 m. above sea-level, and it is the highest mountain in Spain.

A sea of clouds above the Park. In the background, the island of La Palma.

Las Cañadas del Teide national park is located here. It takes its name from the mythical mountains and occupies a wide volcanic egg-shaped hollow, which is 14 km across and covers a total area of 135 km², divided between the municipal districts of La Orotava, Guía de Isora, Santiago del Teide and Icod de los Vinos. This large hollow, whose average height is over 2,000 metres, is split in two by the Los Roques de García massif. Huge walls surround the area along nearly all of its perimeter and which are only broken up by some ravines or natural ways through known as Cañadas (Las Cañadas del Teide) which were used as such by the *guanches,* the first inhabitants of Tenerife, to take their livestock up to the mountain pastures in summer.

Scientists have debated its origin for a long time. According to Carracedo, it is the result of great volcanic activity centred in the area, which took place three million years ago, and which resulted in a large dome between 3,000 and 5,000 m high. Martínez de Pisón and Quirantes in turn believed in the formation of an irregular geological structure, covered with hollows.

Araña spoke of various phases and several eruptions over a period of

Previous double page, the Peak of the Teide in the National Park of Las Cañadas del Teide.

This page, and following double page, different views of the Teide with snow.

time. The large dome theory dominates today –although with certain nuances–, even though the differences of opinion continue where trying to establish the cause of the huge cauldron that surrounds the peak, which is surrounded by a large wall of 12 by 17 km. Nonetheless, the most popular theory is that it caved in.

The volcanic cone of the Teide itself rises up in the northern part of the Park. In reality, it is not just one volcano, but a series of them: Pico Viejo, to the south-east, Montaña Blanca and Pico Cabra. To the west of the cone is Las Narices del Teide, evidence of the last eruption in the area, which took place at the start of the 20th century. There have

Los Roques. Opposite page, El Roque Chinchado, with El Teide in the background.

been various eruptions over recent centuries, with the most important one happening at the end of the 18th century, which left whatis today known as Pico Viejo. Pan de Azúcar or Polón tops the structure, which rises up from the La Rambleta hollow, where fumaroles can still be seen today.

The earth's forces can still leave their mark and the raised

In harmony with its origin, the surface of the park is marked by the results of successive eruptions: solidified tracks, volcanic bombs, lava plains… combining dark, reddish and light shades… It is the site of the so-called *malpaís,* where the range of colours are even more noticeable, as can be seen in Los Azulejos. The Llano de Ucanca

The "Queen's Shoe". ▶

View of the Teide National Park.

temperature that can be seen in those rather deep holes are even further proof.

Many people consider Teide to be the symbol of this Archipelago and it can be seen from most the islands, particularly in winter when it is covered with a layer of snow that coats its slopes and the area around Las Cañadas.

surrounds the foot of the Pico and is a wide plain which is bordered by the aforementioned Roques de García to the north, spectacular lava flows to the west and south and by the Cumbre de Ucanca to the east.

Traces of the *guanches'* habitat, the first inhabitants of Tenerife, can be seen everywhere. Tending

This page and opposite, different views of Ucanca.

livestock was one of their main means of survive and meant that looking after the goats and sheep played a major role in the everyday tasks of the various cantons or menceyatos that the island was divided into. Each of these political units had its own territory, but this exclusivity did not affect the summit area and, in particular, the upland area, including Las Cañadas, which these men considered to be common grazing land.

On the other hand, some students of the religion practised by the first inhabitants of the Canary

Islands, have explained the role that mountains played in their religion: basically, they had a Manichean concept of the Universe, with a deity of good –"Acorán", "Abora", "Orahan"...–, in conflict with an evil one, which in Tenerife's case was "Guayota", who resided inside "Echeide", that is to say, El Teide.

The Park's climate is subtropical high mountain, whose characteristics are defined by the altitude and with average temperature of around 9 °C, although there is a great variation

On these two pages,
we can see...

... the varied geology
of the Park.

These pages, different shapes in the National Park.

between night and day. The insolation level is high and with abundant precipitation, even though it is not spread out evenly through the year, with heavy rain in winter, combined with some equally heavy snowfalls on the northern slopes of Teide. The snow lies for a much shorter period of time in Las Cañadas. A varied, rich and sometimes, unique flora can be expected to be observed in an area dominated by high mountain climatic conditions. The whole of the Park is a garden in spring. The species are small. In fact, there are no trees and any that can be seen have generally been introduced by

Following double page, malpais in Los Azulejos, a good example of the interesting combination of geology and plant life.

man. This is not the case of the Canary Island juniper *(Juniperus cedrus)* which clings to the slopes beside the Canary Island pine *(Pinus canariensis)*. Teide broom *(Spartoctisus supranubius)*, laburnum *(Adenocarpus viscosus)*, red tajinaste *(Echium wildpretii)*, Teide grass *(Nepeta teydea)*, Canary Island cress *(Erysimum scoparium)*, coarse grass *(Descurinia bourgaeana)* and the beautiful Teide violet *(Viola cheiranthifolia)*... live in less rugged areas.

The bird life to be found there includes the rare Egyptian vulture *(Neophron percnopterus)*, the Moorish partridge *(Alectoris barbara*

Red and blue tajinastes on the Teide.

Teide Daisies.

Stone Rose in the natural park that surrounds the Park. ◢

These pages, different views of the vegetation found in the Park and its surroundings.

This page and following double page, lava formations in the North.

Koenigi), the kestrel *(Falco tinnunculus canariensis)*, the peregrine falcon, the wild dove *(Columba livia canariensis)*, the sparrow hawk, the blue chaffinch *(Fringilla teydea teydea)*. The most important reptile is the Black lizard Lacertidae *(Lacerta galloti)*. The mammals are represent by the rabbit *(Oryctolagus cuniculus)*.

The Las Cañadas del Teide Parador, which is open all year, is located within the Park. There is also a Visitors' Centre in El Portillo, which can be reached along the road from La Laguna to La Esperanza, or the road from La Orotava to Las Cañadas. If the visitor takes the southern route to the Park, along the Vilaflor road, he will have to travel through the park to reach the Centre.

This is also the case, if he uses the Chío road. The La Ruleta lookout point is situated 500 m from the Parador.

The Izaña Astrophysical Observatory.

Cable car.

Previous page,
different views of
the San José Mines.

Above, the Hermitage of Las Nieves. Below, hiking is encouraged with well-signposted routes.
However, it is always a good idea to check out all possibilities beforehand.

The Parador Hotel of Las Cañadas del Teide, a good option for staying overnight in the Park and visit it at your leisure.

The north coast from El Sauzal.

Watermill in La Orotava.

Opposite page, the historical quarter of La Orotava.

Festival time in La Orotava. Carpets of flowers opposite the Town Hall during the festival celebration of Corpus Christi (above).

Interior of the House of Los Balcones.

Church of La Concepción in La Orotava.

Previous double page,
the beach of
San Marcos in Icod.

◆ Playa Jardín in Puerto de la Cruz.

San Felipe Castle in Puerto de la Cruz. ◆

View of the Lake Martiánez complex in Puerto de la Cruz. Following double page, the Parrot Park in Puerto de la Cruz. ▶

◆ A view of Garachico.

San Miguel Castle in Garachico. ◆

48

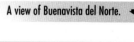

The millennial Drago Tree in Icod de los Vinos.

A view of Buenavista del Norte.